# OLD GLORY
## *Unfurling History*

### Karal Ann Marling

BUNKER HILL PUBLISHING
*In association with the*
Library of Congress

Copyright © 2004 The Library of Congress.
Text copyright © 2004 Karal Ann Marling.
All rights reserved.

First published in 2004 by Bunker Hill Publishing,
6 The Colonnade, Rye Road, Hawkhurst, Kent TN18 4ES, United Kingdom

For the Library of Congress:
W. Ralph Eubanks, Director of Publishing
Amy Pastan, Picture Editor and Project Manager
Aimee Hess, Editorial Assistant

ISBN 1 59373 019 5

Designed by Louise Millar

Printed in China by Jade Productions

Library of Congress Cataloguing in Publication Data
is available from the publisher's office

*Front cover: On a hill overlooking I-95 in Virginia, a veteran waves the flag on September 14, 2001, days after the terrorist attack on the Pentagon. Americans showed the colors in 2001 to pledge their determination to persevere.*

*Title page: Young Patriot, Ashland, Aroostock, ME.*

# Introduction

During the War of 1812, when the city of Baltimore came under attack, a Georgetown lawyer—Francis Scott Key—was enlisted to negotiate the release of an American doctor mistakenly caught up in an enemy search for treasonous British nationals. So, for twenty-five hours on September 13 and 14, 1814, Key found himself aboard a British vessel, watching the bombardment of Fort McHenry, at the mouth of Baltimore's harbor. All day and all night, mortar shells and rockets rained down upon the fort. But at dawn on the second day, Key peered into the golden rays of the morning sun and saw that the American flag still floated bravely above the fort. The attack had failed. Baltimore had been saved. The British threat was over.

On the back of a dog-eared letter he found in his pocket, Francis Scott Key began the poem that more than a century later would become our national anthem. And the verse was all about the flag, the "Star-Spangled Banner," with its "broad stripes and bright stars" flying triumphant over American soil. But what flag did the poet see? Was it the enormous banner made in 1813 by Mary Pickersgill, a professional flag-maker—a flag with fifteen stripes and fifteen stars, each star as large as a person's head? The flag currently under an $18 million reconstruction at the Smithsonian Institution? Or a smaller version, a "storm flag," also stitched by Mrs. Pickersgill and her helpers, intended for use under adverse conditions? The big one, surely, run up the flagstaff after the battle was over, by way of celebration. "O say can you see," wrote Mr. Key, in the first flush of victory. Can you see our Star-Spangled Banner?

*On April 14, 1865, the original flag was reflown over Fort Sumter, in Charleston Harbor, South Carolina. The Confederate attack on the fort and its flag in 1861 began the Civil War.*

*When Washington passed through Trenton, New Jersey, en route to his inauguration in 1789, maidens strewed flowers and flags flew—although not these much later flags, added to the scene by Currier & Ives, ca. 1845.*

As late as 1861, when the official U. S. flag had thirteen stripes (for the original colonies) and thirty-three state stars (Kansas would shortly become the thirty-fourth), patriots were still bewailing the lack of a national anthem. Key's lyric was often disparaged: it was too old-fashioned, "useless" for expressing the passions of a new generation shortly to be engaged in a wrenching Civil War. The flag of Fort Sumter, attacked by the South on April 12, 1861, became an object of veneration after the Union commander evacuated his position, taking the battle-scarred banner with him. This action, historians believe, helped to touch off a "flag mania" that never really went away, turning one symbol of the nation into the American emblem. This enduring "flag mania," and the ever-increasing reverence for the red, white, and blue gave Key's *Star-Spangled Banner* the edge in 1931, when a national anthem was finally adopted. His "useless" old poem, a relic of a forgotten conflict set to the tune of a British drinking song, became America's song.

Critics continue to assail the anthem, however. It's unsingable, they say. Archaic in language. And who ever heard of an anthem built around a question mark? "O say can you see?..." Why are we singing about a flag? Why not *America the Beautiful*, by Katherine Lee Bates, written in 1893 in tribute to the lush Kansas wheatfields and to the majestic mountainscape she saw from Pike's Peak, as a tourist bound for the Chicago World's Fair? A statement about the surpassing loveliness and grandeur of our country. "O beautiful for spacious skies. . . ." And yet, it is hard to sing those words without seeing the flag, dancing across a cloud-dappled sky—a living thing, like a wheatfield rippled by the breeze.

Given the significance attached to the flag, Americans have always suspected that those particular colors must mean something. George Washington has been quoted as saying that the stars came from heaven and the red from the ensign of the Mother Country. The white stripes showed our separation from England: they "shall go down to posterity representing liberty." Glorious rhetoric, but untrue. Washington never said it. Others have argued that red means courage, white means purity, and blue means loyalty. True blue! Or that the red is the blood of Americans who gave their lives for liberty. In fact, the flag has no secret meaning. The flag is what every American wants it to be. Valor, innocence, justice. Joy, hope, and peace. Or simply all of us, together. The U. S. A. Our homeland.

**5**

# Who Invented the American Flag?

Whatever else it may be—symbol, source of deep emotion, an image in a poem—the American flag is a real, tangible thing, too. It is something made out of cloth or, more recently, electric lights, or plastic. Somebody makes it for Wal-Mart, the nation's largest retailer of flags. And once upon a time, somebody designed the first version of the Stars and Stripes. For a century or more, most schoolchildren believed that the "somebody" was Mistress Betsy Ross, seamstress, who lived and worked in a pretty little

*This color print depicts the basic elements of the Betsy Ross story: Mrs. Ross, the delegation, George Washington, the scissors, and the flag. The story was revived in 1932, the bicentennial of Washington's birth, when this picture became popular.*

colonial house on Arch Street, in downtown Philadelphia. The so-called Flag House is now a major local tourist attraction.

According to the story first told in 1870 by her grandson, William Canby, a delegation sent by the Continental Congress called on Mrs. Ross in May of 1776. Would she make a flag for the patriot armies? they asked. She turned to George Washington, whose ruffled shirts she made (the General had also complained that the lack of a single, distinctive flag was crippling the war effort), and asked him to draw her a diagram. When the rough sketch included conventional six-pointed stars like the ones featured on the Washington family crest, she took a scrap of cloth, folded it, and with a single snip produced a more distinctive five-pointed star rarely used in heraldry because of the supposed difficulty of making one. With that clever snip, the job was hers. What we now call the Betsy Ross Flag was soon forthcoming from 239 Arch Street: thirteen alternating stripes of red and white (framed at top and bottom by red ones) and a canton of blue adorned with a circle of thirteen five-pointed stars.

The story is charming and very Victorian. In 1870, Philadelphia was in the midst of preparations to host a great Centennial Exposition, honoring the heroes

*Cleveland artist Archibald Willard created* Fife, Drum, and Flag *(also known as* Yankee Doodle, 1776*) for the U. S. Centennial observances of 1876. Sold as a chromolithograph, the Willard composition shows a Betsy Ross-type flag in the background.*

of 1776. When the splendid fair opened in 1876, so did Betsy's refurbished shop, a new shrine for visiting patriots. In the 1870s, the American woman was expected to be the light of her home, the queen of the domestic circle. Betsy, plying her needle for the nation, was an ideal heroine—submissive, industrious, and homebound—and the perfect match for the great Washington, man of action. If he was the Father of His Country, Betsy became, in effect, the Mother.

THE FLAG THAT HAS WAVED ONE HUNDRED YEARS.

*July 4, 1876:* The flag that has waved one hundred years. *One of many "chromos" sold in the anniversary year, this print was published in Philadelphia as the official Centennial celebration reached its crescendo. In 1876, the flag had 37 stars.*

Now, while Mrs. Ross really was a seamstress and a flagmaker, the story about her collaboration with George Washington is a myth. Congress drew up the specifications for the flag on June 14, 1777 (Flag Day), a year after the supposed *téte à téte* on Arch Street. That resolution mandated the colors, the stars, and the stripes, in language vague enough to permit stars of any kind and stripes arranged as circumstances might dictate. For years afterward, Francis Hopkinson, a sometime poet and artist and one of the signers of the Declaration of Independence, insisted that he had designed that flag and demanded payment, which was never forthcoming. But Betsy Ross, with her parlor, and her scissors, and her gentlemen-callers, makes a better story. As Woodrow Wilson later remarked, "Would that it were true!"

The flag is mythical and a little mysterious, then, but it is also cloth, thread, and colors, arranged according to federal law. In everyday parlance, we are apt to call any flaglike yard goods draped around a convention hall, or the dais of a Fourth-of-July orator, "bunting." In the 1700s, however, the word described a loosely woven woolen fabric, imported from England, that was used specifically to make large flags like Betsy Ross's. Stars, often fashioned from cotton

*In a photograph taken early in the last century, mechanized Betsy Rosses toil over their sewing machines. The U. S. government is the largest consumer of flags, procuring more than 100,000 every year. The oldest commercial flag-making firm is Annin & Co. of New Jersey, founded in 1847.*

muslin, were appliquéd to one side of the blue field; then, the seamstress turned the canton over and cut carefully inside the line of stitches, exposing the cotton. The process was tedious, and flags were costly. During the Civil War, ladies often made flags at home for their local regiments. Commercial firms began to produce so-called "Bible flags," small enough to fit inside the cover of the volume of scripture soldiers carried into battle. Since, in a way, the war was a battle for the flag—would the Stars and Stripes prevail, with

**9**

*May 3, 1955. On the football field at the University of Detroit, members of the campus ROTC clean what was then the world's largest flag, in preparation for upcoming Flag Day exercises.*

its diagrammatic representation of the nation's colonial past and hoped-for unity of 35 fractious state stars?—the flag industry flourished thereafter and homemade flags gradually retreated to grandma's attic.

The colors themselves were standardized for manufacturers in 1934. White is white. The blue is a common shade. But OG Red ("Old Glory red") is a distinctive hue: blood red, the experts say, with the merest

*Los Angeles, 1901: an electric flag—permanent fireworks over the streets of the city. Electric lighting was the last word in public spectacles for a modern age.*

touch of a heavenly blue. A Flag Code, formulated in the 1920s and endorsed by Congress at the end of World War II, mandates how soiled and worn flags are to be disposed of with due reverence. These days, most of us would toss the nylon flag from the front porch into the washer-dryer. And big, expensive flags have been laid out on football fields and scrubbed by volunteers, with no lack of respect for Old Glory. According to the *Guinness Book of World Records*, the largest American flag ever made was fabricated by the Humphrys Flag Co. of Pottstown, Pennsylvania, at the instigation of a gentleman indignant that the current record-holder was a Chinese flag. The Humphrys flag consumed five miles of fabric in the approved colors. It weighed 3,000 pounds. It was so large—255 by 505 feet—that it traveled about for exhibition purposes in its own mobile home. Completed on Flag Day, 1992, it once flew from the Washington Monument, America's biggest, strongest flagstaff. Vast, breathtaking, and as beautiful as America herself, the giant flag billowed forth into a spanking wind. Our Star-Spangled Banner. O say can you see?

# In Search of Uncle Sam

In a tree-shaded cemetery in Troy, New York, lie the mortal remains of Uncle Sam—or so the tombstone says. His real name was Samuel Wilson. A meat packer by trade, he helped to provision troops stationed along the Canadian border during the War of 1812. And on every cask of salted beef destined for the Army, he stamped the letters "U. S.," indicating that it was property of the United States. According to the story handed down in the Wilson family, the recipients of his rations joked that U. S. really meant "Uncle Sam," and the name stuck.

The real story isn't half as interesting. In 1832, a young fellow wrapped in the flag appeared in a political cartoon seated alongside Andrew Jackson, who is attempting to bleed him dry. An allusion to the battle over the Bank of the United States, the cartoon is the earliest instance of the nation being personified by a male figure variously draped or dressed in the Stars and Stripes.

Uncle Sam was still a political icon in 1860, when he figured in Lincoln's campaign for the White House, as a sort of muse of the Republican Party. In the process, Sam also became tall, gaunt, and bewhiskered, a sort of caricature of Abe Lincoln himself. His definitive image was later refined in the

*In the second half of the nineteenth century, patriotic motifs sold a wide variety of products, including coffee. This 1863 label is highly partisan: Sam is trampling a rebel flag underfoot.*

cartoons of Thomas Nast (father of the Republicans' elephant and the Democrats' donkey). Nast experimented with Sam in the pages of *Harper's Weekly* throughout the Civil War era. One of his landmark images—a picture of Santa Claus delivering gifts to Union troops—featured a fat little St. Nick dressed in a fuzzy garment, with striped pants, and a starry shirt, and a belt inscribed with the letters "U. S."

But Uncle Sam and Santa soon parted company, and Sam assumed something of his present-day form, a lanky old gent with a prominent goatee, and an elegant suit cut from the fabric of the American flag: a top hat, stovepipe pants, and a cutaway jacket with long coattails, all in red-and-white stripes and white stars on a field of blue. During Philadelphia's Centennial Exposition of 1876, the new

*The governor of Tennessee, addressing an assembly of Civil War veterans in 1897, a year before this picture was taken, said that Uncle Sam "is the tallest figure on this mundane sphere, and when he steps across the continent and sits down on Pike's Peak, and snorts in his handkerchief of red, white, and blue, the earth quakes and the monarchs tremble on their thrones."*

*This is one of a number of photographs of the same old gentleman—a real-life Uncle Sam—issued for Memorial Day, 1914. Sometimes he wears a GAR medal, identifying him as a Civil War veteran, fifty-odd years after Gettysburg. Codes of conduct governing the display of the flag have consistently opposed apparel decorated in flaglike designs; this figure reminds the viewer of Uncle Sam, without any questionable clothing made from the fabric of Old Glory.*

**13**

*James Montgomery Flagg's definitive Uncle Sam (a self-portrait?) first appeared on the cover of* Leslie's Illustrated Weekly *in February of 1917. As a recruiting poster for the Army, it became the most famous icon of World War I.*

*World War II brought Uncle Sam out of quiet retirement. Here, in the finale of a pageant performed in a New York City grade school in 1943, Sam is just a kid again.*

Sam became a kind of trademark for commercial products made in the U. S. A. Brightly colored trade cards, advertising a spate of newly manufactured goods, used the likeness of Uncle Sam to demonstrate pride in America's new industrial preeminence.

The modern Uncle Sam, pointing a long, bony finger at the potential Army recruit, was a by-product of World War I. Inspired by patriotic fervor, a group of America's top magazine illustrators, all New Yorkers, met weekly at Keene's Chop House to aid the war effort through their art. One of the most prominent members of this so-called Division of Pictorial Publicity was James Montgomery Flagg, renowned for his pictures of movie stars and pretty girls. In this case, Flagg gave up the girls for the stern, demanding old man on what may be the most famous American poster of all time. "I Want You!" growls Flagg's Uncle Sam, eyebrows bristling, as he points directly at the passerby with a ferocious energy.

**15**

# Junior Patriots

"Old Glory," the flag's best-known nickname, comes from a large, 24-star flag owned by a New England sea captain who moved to Nashville in his retirement. In 1860, his wife updated the thirty-six-year-old flag with new stars, and when Union troops liberated the city, Sam Driver's flag was flown in triumph over the Tennessee capitol. Driver called it Old Glory, and the name stuck. Old Glory evoked the endurance of the nation, and the heroism of those who had defended it, from 1776 onward.

Yet America was also the land of perpetual youth and innocence, always new, full of promise. And what better symbol of our tomorrows than a child with a flag? Jeremiah Cohan, an Irish-American vaudevillian, always claimed that his son had been born on July 4, 1878—the offspring of the flag. In truth, George M. Cohan came into the world a day earlier, but myth proved more compelling than fact in the future of the boy who grew up to write "I'm a Yankee Doodle Dandy." He was, as the lyrics of the song insisted, "a real live nephew of my Uncle Sam!" Cohan's popular patriotic songs, including "It's a Grand Old Flag," more than justified his father's prescient fib.

*The little boy represents the Fourth of July, with his flags and clutch of firecrackers. In 1906, he was the ideal American tot: cute and full of mischief.*

Cohan was born in an era that cherished its children, as no generation before had done. Christmas became a child-centered festival: boys and girls were showered with books, and games, and manufactured toys, and whole new industries grew up around gifts for little ones. Currier and Ives's prints and picture magazines were full of adorable girls and mischievous boys, even as reformers began to agitate for the welfare of homeless street urchins and little factory girls, bent over their labor for pennies a day. Children were the Americans of the future. They needed to learn what freedom and democracy meant, and the price that had been paid to secure them. They needed to be nurtured and taught.

The Pledge to the Flag, recited daily in the classroom, was the lynchpin in the patriotic education of the smallest Americans. In the 1880s, veterans of the Civil War promoted the first flag pledge. "We give our heads and hearts to God and our country: one nation, one language, one flag": the wording suggests that the daily flag ceremony was directed in part at the flood of immigrants streaming into urban schools, speaking Russian, Italian, and other tongues. This

*The sheer number of card-mounted photos of children made for sale in the late nineteenth and early twentieth centuries indicates the national obsession with kids. These babies, posed around 1891, are imitating a float in some grand patriotic parade.*

*This little fellow, Master Sidney Arthur Mounteer, had his picture taken in a Chicago photographic studio, wearing the then-popular sailor suit for boys. The painted ocean, the boat, and the flag are props. Sidney could be imitating Christopher Columbus in the aftermath of the 1893 Fair.*

*Ellis Island, 1918: little newcomers celebrate their first American Christmas with toys, stockings, and American flags.*

first pledge was a citizenship exercise for the children of the melting pot.

In 1892, a year before Americans belatedly celebrated the quadricentennial of the voyage of Columbus (an Italian sailor) with a great World's Fair in Chicago, *The Youth's Companion* suggested fresh wording, purged of all reference to language and religion. Who wrote the actual document—"I pledge allegiance to my Flag and the Republic for which it stands, one nation indivisible, with liberty and justice for all"—was the subject of years of claims and counterclaims. Only in 1939 did a committee of the U. S. Flag Association decide that Francis Bellamy, the magazine's circulation manager, was the author. But on October 12, 1892, Columbus Day, over twelve million school kids recited the new text for the first time.

The words have undergone some modification since: in 1923, "my Flag" became "the flag of the United States of America," and in 1954, during the Eisenhower Administration and the Cold War, the

**19**

phrase "under God" was inserted. The biggest change came in the gestures made during the recitation. At the outset, the children began the Pledge with their right hands over their hearts. Then, when they came to the words "my Flag," protocol called for them to fling out the arm toward the flag, palm upraised, in some approximation of an ancient Roman salute. In 1942, when this salute began to look like what the Nazis and Fascists were doing, Congress mandated that the kids should keep their hands firmly on their chests throughout.

In 1943, the Supreme Court determined that no child could be forced to participate in the schoolroom salute: to do so was to

Our Future Friends, 1905. Japanese children on parade wave both American and Japanese flags in a gesture of amity. During the summer of 1905, Secretary of War William Howard Taft met with Japanese Prime Minister Katsura to ratify Japan's protectorate rights in Korea.

Campfire Girls in Juneau, Alaska, 1915, give the old-fashioned Pledge to the Flag salute, right arms extended, right palms facing up.

violate the very liberty celebrated in the Pledge. As the issue continues to be debated today, children continue to delight in the flags they attach to their bicycles for the Fourth of July, the flags they wave at parades, and the flags they raise every morning at summer camp.

# Politics, Presidents, and Flags

The first widespread use of the American flag in the political arena came in 1840, when William Henry Harrison ran for president against the incumbent, Martin Van Buren. Harrison's claim to fame was his military prowess. And, although he hailed from the Virginia Tidewater, he also made much of his log-cabin origins, of being a simple farm boy from the country. During the campaign for the White House—the so-called "Hard Cider and Log Cabin" campaign—supporters of Old Tippecanoe (the creek where Harrison had turned back an Indian attack) dragged log cabins on flag-draped bandwagons through the streets, dispensing artificial cheer from cider barrels. Souvenir items distributed to the faithful carried images of cabins and flags. Campaign banners consisted of flags of various sizes with partisan slogans printed on the white stripes. A lithographed version of the official campaign song, "General Harrison's Log Cabin March," showed both cabin and flag covered with musical notes.

The not-so-subtle point of all the hoopla was to imply that, by comparison, Martin Van Buren was a professional politician and a bit of a fop, whereas Harrison was a real, red-blooded American he-man, sprung from

*The thirty-one star flag, overprinted with the names of the candidates, shows the lasting impact of the 1840 campaign of William Henry Harrison on presidential politics. Throughout much of the nineteenth century, banners were essential to partisan parades, adding life and sparkle to the spectacle. After 1840, the American flag began to displace other colors and symbols.*

humble pioneer stock. Although Harrison won the election, he died only a month after his inauguration, leaving behind as his most lasting legacy the association between the presidency, presidential politics, and the American flag. Official photographs hanging in post offices and courthouses invariably show the sitting president posed before the flag. Televised speeches from the Oval Office, the speeding presidential motorcade, the gala airport welcome: without the presence of the flag, these ceremonial moments would be flat and meaningless.

*William Jennings Bryan, the Democratic Party's candidate, was photographed beside the flag in the fall of 1896, on the campaign trail. He won his party's nomination in July with his "Cross of Gold" speech—one of the most famous public addresses in American history—supporting agrarian interests against the commercial forces of the East. Bryan (and the flag) ran for the presidency three times.*

*William McKinley defeated Bryan in 1896 by supporting the gold standard, high tariffs, and big business. The poster depicts him as a city "gent" in a silk hat being raised aloft by a coalition of factory workers and tycoons. Like Bryan, he is accompanied by the flag.*

**22**

*President Woodrow Wilson, carrying an American flag, makes his way along Pennsylvania Avenue in 1919, in a parade to welcome troops home from World War I. The war inspired a fresh interest in the flag, flag rituals, flag waving, and the use of massed flags on significant public occasions.*

Political figures of all sorts are said to "wrap themselves in the flag" if they utter patriotic platitudes, instead of answering the questions posed to them. To wear the flag is to be above the fray, clothed in the borrowed dignity of the Stars and Stripes—unless the individual in question begs to differ with prevailing opinion. When Congresswoman Patricia Schroeder, who had been elected in 1972 on an anti-war platform, later appeared on a magazine cover cloaked in a capacious flag, she touched off a huge public outcry because she was a feminist and an activist whose views were deemed "countercultural."

Some historians believe that the cultural divide of the 1970s and 80s spawned a flag boom engineered by conservatives. Various corporations, including Reader's Digest and Gulf Oil, distributed millions of flag decals; by 1970, "America—Love It or Leave It" bumper stickers were the rage. Hardhats and

**23**

*A view of the Republican National Convention of 1928 at Madison Square Garden, where a crowd estimated at 22,000 gathered to hear presidential nominee Herbert Hoover speak. There are flags and bunting everywhere; newspapers called this the largest single political gathering in the history of New York City.*

policemen wore flag patches on their work clothes, to show collegiate radicals—the "flag burners"—where they stood. The opposition, meanwhile, wore the flag as a patch on the seat of their jeans, or embellished it with peace signs, or with tiny crosses, standing for those already killed in Southeast Asia. The flag became politicized: intact, and worn as a lapel pin by staffers in the Nixon White House, it was a symbol of the right, whereas, when waved by a leftist "hippie" in a protest parade, it stood for Americans' freedom to dissent.

*Richard Nixon's subsequent resignation in the wake of the Watergate scandal makes the disembodied head of this Charles Winfield Meggs poster, issued for the midterm elections of 1970, seem both sinister and prescient. The President is not the flag (except metaphorically); he or she is not above the law.*

**24**

# Commemorating and Celebrating

Men fought the Civil War, but in the Victorian economics of gender, women did the mourning for those left behind on the battlefields of both North and South. Legend has it that the custom of decorating the graves of the fallen with flowers and flags began, late in the conflict, with pious Confederate widows. By April and May of 1865, Union soldiers were imitating what they had seen and adorning the resting places of comrades who had died far from home. In May of the same year, an abolitionist newly arrived in South Carolina to create schools for freed slaves led a group of African American children in beautifying a nearby military cemetery for federal troops.

By 1869, under the auspices of the Grand Army of the Republic (an organization of Union survivors of the late war), an annual Memorial Day was being held at Arlington National Cemetery on May 30. With feelings still running high, Northern veterans that year staked out the graves of the Confederate dead, lest any tenderhearted lady attempt to honor a rebel. And in the South, therefore, May 30 was widely disdained as a Yankee holiday. Only when animosities began to fade with the passage of time did what was then called "Decoration

*The inscription on the blackboard reads "Decoration Day, May 30, 1899." In this Washington, D. C. school, girls (and a pair of boys) have collected daisies for use in their floral tribute. This is no longer a Northern or a Southern rite. The flags indicate that Decoration Day has become a true national observance.*

Day" become the cornerstone of a national rite of reconciliation, mediated by the sympathies of women, into whose care the flowers, the flags, and the rituals of remembrance were entrusted. Some recent historians posit that women's role in honoring the dead of both camps, and their insistence on a national holiday for that purpose, helped to introduce them into public life in a forceful and unprecedented manner.

*Altoona, Pennsylvania, 1912. For a big, warm-weather parade, the street is decked with flags and fans of bunting, and a group of young scholars (note leader in mortarboard and academic costume) form a "human flag" with their parasols.*

*Ebbets Field, Brooklyn on the first day of the 1914 baseball season—April 14—as a giant flag is hauled out to signal the start of a new year for the National Pastime. Baseball was played by Union troops encamped during the Civil War. Experts insist that the first time the "Star-Spangled Banner" was played to begin a game was in 1862. Whatever the truth, the flag and the song were meant to inspire; many fans think that the last words of the anthem are "Play Ball!"*

26

Although Memorial Day did not become a fixed federal holiday until 1971, it was observed nonetheless, not only with the sad customs of mourning, but as a celebration of unity and patriotic zeal—or a May rite of springtime, reserved for picnics, speeches, home-cranked ice cream, and parades. The public schools were intimately involved in teaching loyalty, history, and Americanism, especially in the 1880s and 90s, with immigration in full flood. With the help of indomitable female teachers, children learned to be one hundred percent Americans by weaving floral tributes for gravesites, wearing caps and sashes made of flag material, reciting great speeches and patriotic poems, and marching through the streets in quasi-military formations, waving little flags as they went. In many American cities and towns, the triumphant, hours-long Memorial Day parade was a high point of the civic year.

In the two decades before World War I, an exuberant, hyperbolic patriotism spread across the landscape. So did a mania for picture postcards. First introduced in earnest at the Chicago World's Fair of 1893, postcards were popular for many reasons: they were cheaper to mail than a letter, required much less literary effort on the part of the sender, and showed a world without televi-

*A "living flag" consisting of 10,000 cadets, formed up on the parade grounds of the U. S. Naval Training Station at Great Lakes, Illinois, in 1917.*

sion and multiplexes something of current events, geographic marvels, and the new department store on Main Street. By 1909, postcard collecting was the hobby of the hour. Collectors even held postcard "showers" in honor of birthdays and weddings: the guests all brought at least twenty of their best cards. A large number of cards featured patriotic motifs, such as Uncle Sams, past presidents, inaugurations, conventions, and

**27**

*A sidewalk entrepreneur in New York City, photographed days after the 2001 attack on the World Trade Center. In the face of tragedy, Americans felt a need to reaffirm their faith in the nation through displaying the flag. At the same time, the flag also spoke of the dead, as a form of memorialization. And the vendor, in the course of doing business, became another living flag.*

historical scenes, all awash in flags. Communities staged scenes for the camera, with an eye to creating popular postcards. Whole towns, for instance, turned out to form "living flags," which became the vogue in picture postcards in 1909 and 1910.

Citizens dressed in red or white or blue stood together so as to duplicate the design of the flag. They were the flag, in fact. Standing in the sunshine, shoulder to shoulder, they became the flag, in an extreme statement of patriotic pride.

# Hail, Columbia!

In the beginning, before the creation of Uncle Sam, there was no universally accepted symbol for the United States of America. In Europe, nations and whole continents were frequently represented as women, carrying various descriptive attributes. Thus, America was an Indian woman with feathers and blankets. After the Revolutionary War, she became particularized by the addition of a soft, pointed cap, the so-called Phrygian cap used in antiquity to distinguish slaves from free citizens. So "America" wore the headgear of freedom, too. Early in the nineteenth century, however, the Indian no longer seemed adequate to describe a country whose proud citizens did not wear buckskins and fringes. In the search for a new personification of the United States, artists turned to a neoclassical maiden, a deity clad in flowing drapery of purest white, and carrying the flag (and sometimes, the cap as well). She was Miss Liberty, destined to become the distaff companion of Uncle Sam.

Liberty was not the irascible old gentleman's mate, to be sure, or even his daughter. For all her feminine grace, she remained ethereal, like the allegorical figures of Alma Mater, or Justice, or Commerce, which still sit primly outside civic buildings, attempt-

*Sheet music for a new song dedicated to the leading Union general in 1861, with lyrics by Cincinnati poet, Mary Farrell Moore. Both the flag and the figure of Columbia enjoyed a vogue in the 1860s, as women's sacrifices on the home front were acknowledged. A parade honoring the inauguration of Abraham Lincoln featured a float that carried thirty-four little girls, representing the states on the American flag. They stopped in front of Lincoln and sang "Hail, Columbia!"*

ing to convey the meaning of abstract concepts with their stony stares. In a sense, for most of the nineteenth century, American women were abstractions, too, seated in the shelter of the home, in nominal charge of virtue, love of beauty, and other similar intangibles.

*This beautiful and mysterious photograph was taken on the beach in Atlantic City some time around 1900. The two proper young ladies, in their demure bathing costumes, seem somehow to belong to the hazy seascape and to the flag that appears out of nowhere behind them.*

Our Flag, *a 1901 pinup, is not an entirely unusual way of representing the body politic! During World War II, any number of saucy pictures aimed at lonely GIs showed glamour girls in provocative poses—and two-piece bathing suits made out of flags.*

Liberty and Columbia were indistinguishable goddesses, until the Statue of Liberty arrived off the Manhattan shoreline in 1886. Then, Lady Liberty became a matronly figure, slightly forbidding with her spiky crown, her gigantic book, and her torch thrust aggressively heavenward. But little Miss Liberty—a.k.a. Columbia or America—remained girlish, forever young and innocent. Eagles swooped happily around her. Caps dangled in the air above her head. Crowned in the victor's olive wreath, and daintily carrying the Stars and Stripes, she was a bright ideal, a vision, a dream. As Liberty, she danced across coins and stamps in her diaphanous gown. As Columbia (a

*The little girl posing for an art class in a Washington, D. C., school at the end of the nineteenth century is wearing what was called a "parade dress." Homemade or store-bought, flag middies were popular for both child spectators and participants in parades on the Fourth of July, Memorial Day, and other gala occasions. Like Columbia, she wears the Phrygian cap of liberty. In her heyday, Shirley Temple posed for publicity photos in similar outfits.*

feminized version of "Columbus," and a popular name for the U. S. among early poets), she inspired several of the republic's most popular songs.

"Hail, Columbia!" was written for Gilbert Fox, a performer slated to play Philadelphia in 1798, during a bruising political battle between Federalists and Republicans over passage of the Alien and Sedition Acts. With the city divided into hostile camps, Fox turned to a friend, Joseph Hopkinson (son of Francis Hopkinson, who claimed to have designed the flag), for a patriotic number that might appeal to both

*31*

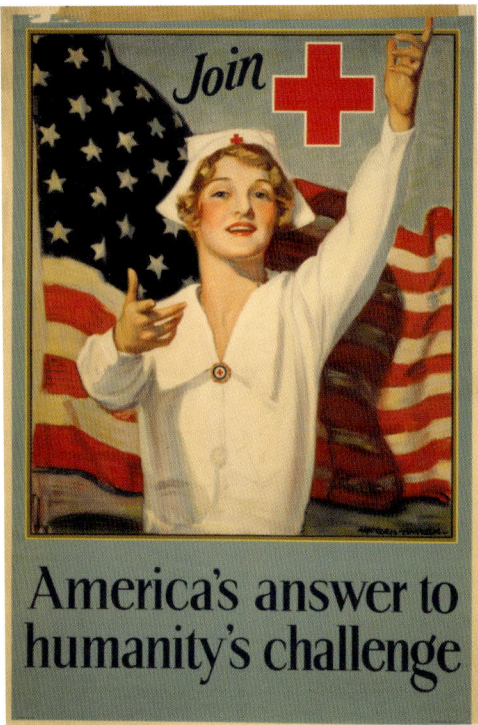

Join

America's answer to humanity's challenge

*World War I was, perhaps, the great age of the American poster. The heroic nurse, reaching out her arms in appeal before a waving flag, stands at the opposite end of the spectrum from the patriotic pinup. The position of her arms and the cry on her parted lips suggest freedom and equality for women, without the need for allegorical disguise.*

factions. Using an older tune, Hopkinson added new words, saluting Columbia: "Hail! Columbia, happy land!" Although the winsome lass in white is nowhere mentioned, the lyrics do confirm a kind of split identity for the nation: a feminine principle, lauded and then discarded in the remainder of the song,

which dwells on great deeds by great men.

Fox's ditty was a great hit, so much so that another singer, David T. Shaw, in search of a song guaranteed to bring his audience to their feet at the conclusion of each concert, enlisted the help of actor Thomas Becket. In 1843, the pair—in open rivalry with "Hail, Columbia!"—wrote "Columbia, Gem of the Ocean" virtually overnight. Ironically, this song also debuted in Philadelphia to a tumultuous response. In Shaw's verses, Columbia is a place, "the home of the brave and the free," whereas Liberty is a sort of personage, who bears the flag, and the wreaths of victory, and the stars of glory.

However tentative the identification between womanhood, nationhood, and the flag may have been before the Nineteenth Amendment was finally ratified in 1920, it nonetheless persisted. John Greenleaf Whittier's story-poem, "Barbara Frietchie," purports to describe an incident that took place during the Civil War in Frederick, Maryland. As Stonewall Jackson's troops file past her house, the 96-year-old widow dangles the Stars and Stripes from an upstairs window in a gesture of defiance. A Confederate soldier fires at the banner and hits it. But the old lady catches the flag, shakes it at the foe, and scolds the rebels: " 'Shoot if you must this old gray head,/ But spare your country's flag,' she said."

Throughout the 1860s and 70s, the story was hotly debated. Testimonials were solicited from natives of Frederick. No less a figure than Dorothea Dix went to Maryland to confirm the incident with the good lady's

*At the headquarters of the National Woman's Party, members salute the success of the drive to give women the vote, with palms raised in the accepted manner of the day. Like Columbia, Liberty, and America, women had become real, first-class citizens.*

relatives. Sensibly, in 1876, as the veracity of the Betsy Ross story was being tested, a lady reader wrote to the *Philadelphia Press*, on the occasion of the Centennial Exposition, arguing that if the Barbara Frietchie legend was not true, it *ought to be*. It made no difference, fact or pious lie. Women were every bit as patriotic as men, even though they were barred from the field of battle. Miss Liberty sewed the uniforms and the quilts (often with flag designs) and the flags themselves. Columbia rolled the bandages. Together, they tended the home fires. In all their various costumes—matron, sprite, goddess, granny—women were, indeed, America.

**33**

# Showing the Colors

When should Old Glory be flown? And how? According to a Flag Code passed by Congress in 1942, there is a strict etiquette about its display (daylight only, unless proper illumination is provided), treatment (a formula for folding the cloth into a tight triangle), and disposal (in a dignified way, preferably by burning). But the regulations fail to reckon with the variety of reasons for which Americans are prone to wave their flag and the extreme conditions under which showing the flag becomes an urgent necessity.

First among these unusual circumstances is exploration—finding what nobody else has ever seen before. Beginning with "Ham" the chimp, in January of 1961, American astronauts blasted into space with flag patches on their pressure suits and pocketsful of tiny flags for souvenirs. After the crew of Apollo 11 landed on the moon on July 20, 1969, one of the important tasks on their checklist was to plant the Stars and Stripes on the lunar surface. Neil Armstrong and Buzz Aldrin did so, with difficulty, in the obdurate terrain. And the flag needed to be stiffened with wire, because there

*July 20, 1969. The crew of Apollo 11 leaves human footprints on the moon. The American flag, stiffened by wire to wave in the airless atmosphere, marks a high point in NASA's mission to the planets.*

COL. FRÉMONT
PLANTING THE AMERICAN STANDARD ON THE ROCKY MOUNTAINS.

*John C. Frémont, the "Pathfinder," launched his campaign for the presidency in 1856 on the strength of his heroic exploits as a surveyor and explorer of the West. This image is a proof for a banner or poster in support of his unsuccessful run on the Republican ticket. A similar likeness of Frémont with his flag appeared on a postage stamp in 1898.*

is no wind on the moon to let it wave triumphantly over the precise spot where mankind took its "one great leap" into tomorrow. Later, after six more crews had set foot on the gray lunar grit, one of their number took pains to explain that the flag did not represent a territorial claim. Instead, it was an expression of gratitude to Americans for their support of the space program. The flag stood for the allegiance and dedication of the more than 400,000 scientists and technicians whose hard work carried humanity toward the stars.

At the other end of the historical spectrum, Meriwether Lewis and William Clark also undertook the first expedition into what would become the western United States amply equipped with flags. When they left St. Louis in 1804, they carried with them 15-star flags in three sizes. Some were flown over their camp. But in 1805, Lewis described an incident in which the party presented a flag to a Native American tribe as a gesture of peace and friendship. On his 1806 expedition to the southern plains, Zebulon Pike used the same tactics to pacify potentially hostile Indians. Once, he insisted that a village haul down a Spanish flag and raise the American banner instead, until he realized that the inhabitants were afraid of the Spaniards. Then Pike returned their flag and gave them the Stars and Stripes instead, in an act of amity.

John C. Frémont's surveying expeditions in the Rockies in the 1840s saw him planting flags on the tallest mountains in sight, for a variety of reasons: sheer exuberance, as symbolic traffic signs directing new settlers to the Pacific Coast, and as grand gestures that enhanced his heroic image. Frémont even ran up a flag of his own devising atop Pike's Peak. The stripes were fine, but in the canton the stars were replaced by an eagle

**35**

(embroidered by his wife) holding a peace pipe in its talons. The message was plain. Although Frémont was a tireless advocate of expansion and Manifest Destiny, he wished it known that he came in peace.

One of the strangest episodes in the history of American exploration came in 1909, when Admiral Richard Peary returned to New York from the Arctic claiming to have reached the North Pole on April 6. But shortly thereafter, Dr. Frederick A. Cook surfaced, insisting that he had arrived there by a more difficult route almost a year earlier. Peary, for his part, said that Cook was a fraud—that he, Peary, had raised the Stars and Stripes there first and left behind a small silk flag to mark the location. Both men brought home photographs, fogged by

*The expedition camp of Frederick Cook, with two members of his party posing with a flag flying over their igloo. The Brooklyn-born Dr. Cook began his treks to the Arctic in 1891, as surgeon to Robert Peary's team. Later, Cook became his competitor. He claimed to have reached the North Pole in 1908, a year before Peary.*

*In 1917, the textile workers at the Amoskeag Mill in Manchester, New Hampshire, determined to make the largest American flag ever produced. The finished flag strictly followed an Executive Order of October 12, 1914 in regard to proportions and colors. The finished product weighed 200 pounds and the plant boasted that never, during the process of weaving, dyeing, cutting, sewing, and finishing had any part of the flag touched the ground.*

the cold, showing members of their respective parties (although not the leaders) posing with flags in endless snowfields. By the end of the year, nonetheless, Cook's claim had been widely discredited because, on an earlier expedition to Alaska, he had filed a bogus report of having scaled Mount McKinley in rubber boots. Whether Peary actually stood upon the shifting icepack at the Pole is still open to question. But Cook's story seems to be a great American hoax, in the style of P. T. Barnum.

**37**

*Ships show the colors for ready identification in foreign ports or, in this case, to honor an historic vessel. Photographed in 1909, this is the Norwich, the oldest steamboat in the world, according to the caption, built in 1836.*

The Flag Code seems not to have considered exigent circumstances, like lunar landings and polar treks. In addition to rules on how to fly flags on poles, it also mandates how to hang a flag against a flat surface. If vertical, then the field of stars ought to be at the top, to the viewer's left. If horizontal, in the same manner: stars up and to the left, stripes down. But under no circumstances should the American flag be used to advertise anything. Nor should it

*The Boy Scouts of America were among the most visible patriots of the early twentieth century. During World War I, troops of scouts held martial drills on the downtown streets of many cities, including New York, where they raced down Broadway after war was declared on Germany with huge American flags streaming behind them. They were also among the 66 organizations active in the 1923 National Flag Conference, which codified rules for handling and showing the colors.*

*This poor, unpainted house outside White Plains, Georgia, showed the hopeful patriotism of its inhabitants in 1941, as World War II began.*

constitute an element of costume. For the same reason that explorers run up their flags in excitement, in urgency, and in sheer exhaustion, Americans tend to break the rules out of an inner necessity to see Old Glory in times of extreme emotion. Shirts. Ads. A symbol on the moon. It's still our flag.

*39*

# I Love a Parade!

Before the coming of television, parades were a vital part of American life. They were entertainment, visual spectacle. They gave the countless Americans who had taken music lessons as youngsters a chance to toot that horn and bang that drum. They stirred up strong emotions and martial fervor. Often lasting for hours in big cities, parades—like the Labor Day Parade—included as a marcher just about anybody who worked for a living, with their families looking on proudly. On Memorial Day, kids cheered when tanks and artillery rumbled down Main Street. Parade floats, which began as decorated wagons, served both to educate and amuse, with scenes from history and literature. Parades were opportunities for communities to come together en masse, to celebrate themselves and their stake in the town, the state, and the nation.

Many of the functions of the parade have been absorbed by other media. We can see politicians' pictures in the newspapers, and see famous parades, such as the Macy's Thanksgiving Day extravaganza, on TV, where dance routines are tailored to the

*A 1917 Memorial Day poster honors all the veterans of America's wars. The American Revolution is represented by two modern scouts with fife and drum, leading a grand parade.*

*A 1932 parade in Washington, D. C. Two hundred and sixty sailors carry what was then the world's largest flag.*

camera. But one element of the old-fashioned, flag-draped Fourth of July parade that television can't capture is the bone-jarring, heart-stopping noise of a big brass band. Musicologists say that between 1895 and 1918, "March King" John Philip Sousa, was responsible for 26 of the 40 top sheet music and wax cylinder hits. The circus, the concert in the park, the holiday parade: no important civic occasion seemed quite com-

**41**

*The parade—this one by water—can also be a protest: the leading elements of "Coxey's Army" of unemployed workmen stormed Washington, seeking federal public works and relief in the aftermath of the Panic of 1893.*

plete without the blare and the boom of the band, and Sousa was the most famous bandleader of them all. No fair could properly open, no ribbon could be cut with impunity unless Sousa was there in person, with his own world-famous band.

In the 1890s, while on an ocean voyage back from Europe, Sousa learned of the death of a trusted friend, who managed the band's affairs. As he paced the deck of the liner, a tune began to play in his head. By the time he reached New York, "The Stars and Stripes Forever" was finished. This new anthem became a national sensation. Sousa played it at every engagement, and so did every other band. By World War I, it was the

**42**

best known patriotic march tune in the land. A popular biographical film on the life of Sousa, made in 1952, was called Stars and Stripes Forever. In 1932, just after the elderly John Philip Sousa conducted a rehearsal of his beloved march in a town in Pennsylvania, he died. In 1987, "The Stars and Stripes Forever" was named the "Official March of the United States."

*Suffragettes on parade in New York City, May 6, 1912, with a baby carriage in the lead.*

*Carrying the flag in a parade can be hard work, as the expressions on the faces of these weary GIs attest.*

Ticker-tape parades for heroes, kiddie parades with dogs pulling little red wagons, parade ground exercises: whether on tape or snappily performed by professionals or massacred by a junior high school band, the official march—Sousa's flag march—is always heard when the parade goes by.

*A Ku Klux Klan parade in Washington in 1926, at the peak of the organization's power and influence. Klan members march under the banner of Americanism.*

**43**

# Battle Flags

The first and most persistent use of flags, and banners, and standards has been to distinguish one foe from another on the field of battle—and to declare victory. A flag run up on the highest point of the battlefield stands for conquest, possession. Somebody has lost. And somebody—the one with the flag—has won. Taking the enemy's flag, or desecrating it, is also a confirmation of victory.

*This frontline conference between the President and his general in the fall of 1862 in Antietam, Maryland, shows the flag as an item of homely domesticity in the field.*

*American soldiers who carried Old Glory on the field of battle in the nineteenth century might have disputed the adage that "The Pen is Mightier Than the Sword."*

*"Teddy" Roosevelt and his Rough Riders pose atop a hill they have taken during the Battle of San Juan in 1898. This is an image of victory.*

Flags captured during the Civil War are still a bone of contention among several states today; Minnesota, for example, has steadfastly refused to return to a Southern capitol a flag captured more than a hundred years ago. Flags made by the loving hands of wives and mothers acquired special meaning in the 1860s. At the same time, however, there were no clear codes of honor that governed the disposition or usage of flags. A photograph taken by Alexander Gardner at the Battle of Antietam is a case in point. Lincoln and General George McClellan sit in the latter's tent, where the flag is being used as a tablecloth. Confederates treating the same flag so cavalierly, however, were expressing contempt for the Union. During Christmastime festivities in a Southern city in 1862, it was reported that Jefferson Davis's party attended a wedding at which the guests danced on floors carpeted with the Stars and Stripes.

In the spring of 1945, the most famous combat photograph of World War II used the flag in yet another way: as a sign that the tide of battle was turning. Taken by Associated Press photographer Joe Rosenthal, the picture shows five Marines and a Navy corpsman raising the American flag atop Mount Suribachi during the fierce battle for the Pacific island of Iwo Jima.

*Sidney Riesenberg, one of the greatest illustrators of the World War I era, captured the danger and desperation of trench warfare in the urgent brushwork that impels the young doughboy out of the poster, clutching at his flag.*

**45**

After days of heavy naval barrage, American troops came ashore under withering fire from an enemy dug into caves that honeycombed the island. Casualties on the beach were heavy. And moving inland under fire was literally a desperate, uphill battle against entrenched Japanese positions.

In the midst of the chaos, a small scouting party had managed to reach the top of the mountain, where they raised the flag to rally their comrades below. But military brass meeting offshore decided that to stiffen American resolve in the face of heavy resistance, a bigger flag was needed, visible from every part of the island. So up went a second patrol, straight into the enemy's stronghold, trailed by Rosenthal and his camera. Up went a larger flag to inspire fighting on every corner of Iwo Jima. And Rosenthal's photograph went back to newspapers all across the country, to rally a weary home front with the prospect of ultimate victory.

*Of the group of six young Americans photographed by Joe Rosenthal as they raised the flag over the Japanese-held island of Iwo Jima in March, 1945, only three came home to tell the story.*

**46**

*Issued in the aftermath of the
most unpopular war in American
history, this poster reminded the
nation that Americans fought and
died under their flag in Viet Nam,
and are entitled to proper respect
for their sacrifices.*

47

*A celebration of the Japanese surrender in 1945 in Chinatown, New York City brought out the victory flags.*

The picture affected those who saw it in a visceral way. In their rumpled dungarees, the figures looked like classical warriors in some ancient frieze, the embodiment of bravery and heroism. Because the faces of the young Marines were hidden from view, it was easy to imagine that this one or that one was *my* son, *my* brother, *my* sweetheart. That the long trek to the Japanese homeland was almost over. That the final victory was at hand. Joe Rosenthal's photograph won the Pulitzer Prize. It was reproduced in every conceivable medium, including postage stamps and ice cream molds. No bond rally was complete without a group of veterans or scouts imitating the poses of the picture. The military tracked down the three survivors of the group that raised the flag and sent them on tour to sell war bonds and to reassure the public that America's fighting men would carry the day.

Eventually, in 1954, in the midst of the Cold War, a colossal bronze statue recreating the Iwo Jima flag-raising was erected in Washington, D. C., as if to warn the world that American courage had not faltered in the years since Old Glory waved fitfully over that faraway battlefield. The bronze figures remain frozen in place forever. But the flag they struggle to plant on that mountain—a real red, white, and blue American flag—billows forth in the breeze off the Potomac River, a living thing, a memory that springs to mind whenever the flag is kissed by the wind.

# Flags Sell Soap, Sodas, Songs, Stamps . . .

*Part politics, part commerce, this 1854 label for a bar of Boston-made soap alludes to a popular anti-immigrant, nativist movement—the "Know Nothings"—with the image of Native Americans guarding the flag.*

Although there exists a persistent, nagging suspicion that using the flag to sell one's wares might not be a suitable fate for the nation's primary symbol, Old Glory and commerce have been uneasy partners almost from the beginning. By the time of George

Washington's death in 1799, a full line of dishware, prints, and other flag-draped Washingtoniana was already on sale. In the nineteenth century, the line expanded to include coffee and tobacco tins, cigar bands, and bottled vinegar, tricked out in stars, stripes, and all the right colors. And despite vigorous objections in the 1960s and 70s to any form of suspected flag desecration, including flag patches on the clothing of

*Russell Lee, one of the best-known Farm Security Administration photographers of the 1930s, took this picture of a newsstand in July of 1942 in Eureka, California, for the Office of War Information. The flag covers run the gamut from wholesome family fare to patriotic cheesecake.*

protesters, some modern-day businesses have become wholly identified with the Stars and Stripes. Cars are routinely offered for sale under yards of bunting and hundreds of little flags. The place to stop for pancakes and burgers is marked by a giant flag, beckoning drivers off the interstate. Flag-strewn newspaper ads for Presidents' Day sales offer women's coats and children's underwear at bargain prices.

One of the most ambitious such sales campaign took place on July 4, 1942, less than a year after the attack on Pearl Harbor (and the year in which Congress officially recognized the Pledge of Allegiance!). To sell both magazines and war bonds, publishers joined forces with the Treasury Department: the plan was to adorn the covers of almost 300 popular magazines with stirring images of Old Glory. The motto of the enterprise

**DAVIS DRUG COMPANY**
FORT SMITH, ARKANSAS

*A photograph of the lavishly appointed interior of a drugstore soda fountain in Arkansas, ca. 1915, is typical of post-card images advertising all kinds of business establishments. The flags could indicate that the picture was taken on a patriotic holiday, but such decorations were also symbols of a grand opening, any time.*

*Santa Claus and the American flag: two of the nation's most potent symbols join forces on a rolling post office in Washington, D. C.*

was "United We Stand," and many editors used that text beneath a picture of a flag to foster grassroots unity among all Americans, whether their favorite reading material was *Vogue*, or *Life*, or *Poultry Tribune*.

But interpretations of the meaning of the flag were as varied as the readership of the periodicals on which it appeared. *House Beautiful* showed a happy family, raising the flag over the tidy yard of their new Cape Cod-style home. *Modern Beauty Shop* featured the photograph of a woman, seen from the rear, saluting the flag; naturally, her hair was coifed to perfection in an obvious permanent wave. Even comic books got into the act, with Porky Pig, Donald Duck, Superman, and Captain Marvel all toting flags.

Advertisers and patriots alike have always sensed the power of that simple design of stars and stripes to arouse strong feelings in the hearts of Americans. When designing packaging for supermarket products, Madison Avenue gurus have agonized from time to time over whether red appeals more strongly to the consumer than blue, but nobody has ever doubted that red, white, and blue, arranged in some flaglike configuration, can sell almost anything: ideas, candidates, magazines—or popsicles.

**51**

# Half-Mast: Flags of Sorrow

As a sign of mourning and respect for the dead, the flag may be raised to the top of its pole and then lowered to half-mast, slowly and reverently. Over the White House, the Stars and Stripes were displayed in this manner for the first time in April, 1841, to mark the the death of President William Henry Harrison, a month into his term. His coffin rested there, too, draped in the flag. And so began a great national pageant of official mourning, reenacted for presidents and humble citizens alike. When Abraham Lincoln was assassinated in April of 1865, less than a week after Lee surrendered to Grant at Appomattox, he became a martyr to the cause of Union. Flags were lowered all along the route of the train that bore his body back to Illinois.

Poet Walt Whitman described Lincoln's last journey home as sanctified "with the pomp of inloop'd flags." Every day, at a military cemetery somewhere in America, an honor guard solemnly folds the flag that served as a coffin's blanket and presents it to a widow, a mother, a family, with the thanks "of a grateful nation." Our flag is the pall of heroes, the shroud of patriots. The flag, said Henry Ward Beecher in an 1861 speech to a Brooklyn regiment bound

*The Grand Review of the Union Army, Washington, D. C., May, 1865. The flag flies at half-mast a month after Lincoln's death and black crepe still dangles from the columns.*

for the battlefield, "is not a painted rag. It is a whole national history. It is the Constitution. It is the Government. It is the Nation." Often, it is a sorrowing nation—or an angry one.

Deliberate misuse of the flag shows contempt for the "Nation" of which Beecher spoke. The act itself is a source of both sorrow and anger, whether it is performed by flag-burning Iranian students in the 1970s, Iraqis in 2004, or American war protesters throughout the twentieth century. The first

American citizen ever prosecuted for torching the flag was a self-styled New York revolutionary who was arrested in 1916 because he had used Old Glory in an anti-war cartoon. On the day before his scheduled trial, the defendant made matters worse by burning a flag in public, and was sentenced to 60 days in jail.

With feelings running high on both sides of the debate over American participation, the World War I era was a particularly volatile period for demonstrations honor-

*An American victim of the sinking of the* Lusitania *in May, 1915. The British liner, carrying many American passengers, was attacked by a German submarine without warning. A total of 1,198 died, including 128 Americans. The incident helped to fuel public enthusiasm for joining the war against Germany.*

*Flag-covered coffins of the dead, brought back from Cuba for burial in Arlington National Cemetery in December, 1899, at the end of the Spanish-American War. The war began in February, 1898, when the U. S. battleship* Maine *blew up in Havana harbor, presumably because of sabotage. In 1976, a commission led by Admiral Hyman Rickover concluded that spontaneous combustion in a coal bunker caused the blast.*

ing the flag—or challenging the nation for which it stood. Immigrants, the ignorant, and some *bona fide* radicals all came in for beatings and arrest for handling flags in ways deemed inappropriate. George M. Cohan, on the other hand, came to realize that "many a bum show has been saved by the flag!" In 1968, Abbie Hoffman was arrested for wearing a store-bought flag shirt to a hearing conducted by the House Un-American Activities Committee. In 2001, in the aftermath of the events of 9/11, everybody wore the flag as a shirt, a jacket, a lapel pin, a cap. Not to wear the flag was now un-American!

**53**

*Robert F. Kennedy, brother of the late president, was gunned down in the kitchen of the Ambassador Hotel in Los Angeles in June, 1968, during his own presidential campaign. After services at St. Patrick's Cathedral, the funeral cortege made the 226-mile trip from New York to Washington by train. All along the right-of-way, mourners gathered with flags to express their grief.*

*The Pentagon in the aftermath of September 11, 2001. The flag stands for sorrow, shock, defiance, and determination.*

Americans have often reacted against abuse of the flag (and what it stands for) by showing greater reverence for it. The courts have held that use or misuse of the Stars and Stripes constitutes a form of speech, protected by the Constitution. Constitutional amendments to exempt the flag from the free speech provisions of the Bill of Rights have not, thus far, made much headway. Tastes change. Perceptions change, too. In 1990, comic Roseanne Barr was widely faulted for singing the national anthem badly at a baseball game between the San Diego Padres and the Cincinnati Reds. At the conclusion of her screeching, Barr then grabbed her crotch (in the manner of ballplayers caught in the act by the indiscreet eye of the TV camera). Former opera star Robert Merrill, who sang the "Star-Spangled Banner" at ballparks during nine presidencies, took particular exception to her performance. "It was like burning the flag," he insisted. But it wasn't, was it? Roseanne Barr, meaning to be satirical, was at best foolish. The joke was lame. She was not seeking, by her gesture, to defame the nation, its war dead, or its Founding Fathers. Nor did she accomplish much except, perhaps, to make Major League Baseball pay more attention to those chosen for anthem duty.

The ideal flag ripples in the breeze, against a clear blue sky, or, in times of crisis, slips down the staff but still billows out smartly, as if to comfort the sorrowful with the promise that America will persist, despite tragedy and tears. The flag that was dangled by construction crews from the facade of the Pentagon, near the gaping hole where terrorists had crashed a passenger jet into the building, was nothing fancy. It hung a little askew, off to one side, a kind of commentary on the death and ruin nearby. It spoke of sorrow, of anger, of frantic haste, of a steely resolve to make things right again. It was the Nation. The Government. The Constitution. It was all of us.

# It's My Flag, Too!

Among its many uses, the flag is a sign of belonging: those who honor it express their essential kinship with one another, even when the citizen who flies the flag has been denied the rights enjoyed by his neighbors. To slaves, to Native Americans, to women of the nineteenth century, the flag represented hope and aspiration. To African Americans in the wake of the Civil Rights Movement, it has often carried a message of reproach, of promises unfulfilled. To a protester at home or abroad, the flag is challenge to America

*Native Americans of twenty nations participate in a flag-raising ceremony on the site of Old Fort Union, ca. 1910. Built in 1828 by the American Fur Company near the junction of the Missouri and the Yellowstone Rivers, Fort Union was the trading center for the whole of the Great Plains, until it was abandoned in 1867. The American flag was a favorite motif among Plains Indian artists.*

*The American Red Cross distributes boots to war refugees from the city of Venice in 1918. The flag identifies the donors of the footgear.*

to live up to the ideals it expresses in those stars and stripes. Sometimes, the flag carries the weight of a terrible sadness; the tanks that attacked the Branch Davidian compound in 1993, under circumstances that still arouse moral debate, flew Old Glory as they hurtled toward an inferno on the Texas plains. The astronauts lost in the Challenger disaster of 1986 marched off to their rendezvous with eternity in uniforms bedecked with the flag. Like America herself, the flag is all things to all people: a prayer, a faith, an ideal gone wrong, a promise, a bitter disappointment.

It stands for freedom—and brute force. For unity—and ancient divisions. For solace—and anger. It is a prop for George Patton, and Bruce Springsteen, and Betsy Ross—and hippies storming the Pentagon. It

*A banner flying from the window of the NAACP (National Association for the Advancement of Colored People) headquarters on Fifth Avenue, New York City, announces another lynching of a black American, 1936. In ironic contrast, the American flag is visible just beneath the banner.*

belongs to the President—and to the smallest Girl Scout. To the military—and to the ballpark and the church on the corner. It flies above the tombs of our greatest heroes—and is saluted by our newest citizens, drawn from the dispossessed of the world.

*Japanese-American children wave a flag and give the "V for victory" sign as their train leaves Seattle, bound for a detention camp, March 30, 1942.*

*At the end of their five-day march from Selma to Montgomery, 25,000 civil rights activists wave American flags before the Alabama State Capitol, March, 1965. The procession, led by Dr. Martin Luther King, Jr. made the 54-mile trek to assert the right of blacks to vote without interference in Alabama. While driving some marchers back to Selma, Viola Liuzzo, a Detroit woman, was attacked and killed by an angry white mob.*

Franklin Roosevelt put the flag on the cartons in which Lend Lease supplies were shipped to the Allies during World War II; pizza delivery services nationwide put it on their boxes after 9/11. The flag reminds, rebukes, celebrates, and mourns. The flag is all of us. Good. Bad. Living. Dead. Old Glory is the best in us, and sometimes the worst. But, in the end, it is us. You and me. We are the flag.

*61*

# Image Reproduction Numbers and Acknowledgments

The following list provides the creators and reproduction numbers for Library of Congress items in this publication, where such information is available. Color transparencies are generally indicated by the prefix LC-USZC4, while the prefix LC-USZ62 generally indicates a black and white negative. Color copy transparencies or black and white prints may be ordered directly from the Library's Photoduplication Service, Washington, D.C., 20540-5230 (telephone 202-707-5640). Information about the Library's Photoduplication Service may also be accessed at the Library's Internet address, http://www.loc.gov. All items listed below are from the Library's Prints and Photographs Division. The Library's general telephone number is 202-707-5000.

Front cover: LC-DIG-ppmsca-02129, by Dylan Moore, photo courtesy the photographer

Title page: LC-USW3-030609-E, by John Collier

3: LC-USZ62-2461

4: LC-USZC2-3162, by Currier & Ives

6 and back cover, top: LC-USZC4-9905, by J. L. G. Ferris

7: LC-USZC4-694, by Archibald Willard

8: LC-USZC4-6287, by Dominique C. Fabronius

9: LC-USZ62-22192

10: LC-USZ62-103791, photo courtesy AP/ Wide World Photos

11: LC-USZ62-46720, by John Best

12: LC-USZC4-2074, by Kilburn & Mallory

13: (Left) LC-USZ62-77900, by Joseph Randall Blanchard (Right) LC-USZ62-58599

14: LC-USZC4-2736, by James Montgomery Flagg

15: LC-USW3-017674-E, by Marjory Collins

16: LC-USZ62-24045, by F. A. Loomis

17: LC-USZC4-5587, by W. T. Barnum

18 and back cover, middle: LC-USZ62-82748, by W. M. Morrison

19: LC-USZ62-83221, by Paul Thompson

20: (Left) LC-USZ62-53239, (Right) LC-USZ62-132420

21: LC-USZC4-2569 by H. C. Howard

22: (Left) LC-USZC2-6259, by Geo. H. Van Norman (Right) LC-USZC2-201

23: LC-USZ62-41790, by W. C. Cox

24: (Top) LC-USZ62-66068 (Bottom) yan 1a39134, by Charles Winfield Meggs, photo courtesy Yanker Poster Collection

25: LC-USZ62-4555, by Frances Benjamin Johnston

26: (Top) LC-USZ62-69822, by A.R. Bardsley (Bottom) LC-USZC4-4708 by George Grantham Bain

27: LC-USZ62-70908

28: LC-DIG-ppmsca-01744, by Kevin Bubriski, photo courtesy the photographer

29: LC-USZC4-1739

30: (Left) LC-USZ62-57867, by J. Fowser (Right) LC-D418-30969

31: LC-USZ62-68425, by Frances Benjamin Johnston

32: LC-USZC4-10138, by Hayden Hayden

33: LC-USZ62-14447, by Harris & Ewing

34: Photo courtesy NASA

35: LC-USZ62-49597

36: LC-USZ62-127912

37 and endpapers: LC-USZ62-108050, by Harlan A. Marshall

38: (Left) LC-USZ62-54107 (Right) LC-USZ62-95814, by William Herman Rau

39: LC-USF35-603, by Jack Delano or Marion Post Wolcott

40: LC-USZC4-6266

41 and back cover, bottom: LC-USZ62-39860, by Underwood & Underwood

42: LC-USZ62-10919, by R.S. Balser

43: (Top left) LC-USZC4-5585, by American Press Association (Bottom left) LC-USZ62-96154, by National Photo Company (Right) LC-USW3-029832-E, by Esther Bubley

44: (Left) LC-USZ62-63487 (Top right) LC-B8171-0602, by Alexander Gardner (Bottom right) LC-USZC4-7934, by William Dinwiddie

45: LC-USZC4-9850, by Sidney H. Riesenberg

46: LC-USZ62-64011, by Joe Rosenthal, Associated Press, photo courtesy AP/Wide World Photos

47: LC-USZC4-6638, by Frederick Schneider, photo courtesy Posters, Inc.

48: LC-USZC4-4844, photo courtesy AP/Wide World Photos

49: (Left) LC-USZC4-5004 (Right) LC-USF34-073275-E, by Russell Lee

50: LC-USZ62-71954

51: LC-USZ62-99592, by National Photo Company

52: LC-B8171-7748, by Mathew Brady

53: (Left) LC-USZ62-41746 (Right) LC-USZ62-84435, by George Grantham Bain

54: LC-L901-68-3791, by Paul Fusco, Look Magazine Collection, photo courtesy Paul Fusco/Magnum Photos, Inc.

55: LC-DIG-ppmsca-02135, by Lana Lawrence, photo courtesy the photographer

57: LC-USZ62-55797, by George Grantham Bain

58: LC-USZ62-77600

59: LC-USZC4-4734

60: LC-USZ62-41516

61: LC-USZ62-126850, by United Press International, photo courtesy Corbis

64: LC-USZ62-35488, by J. R. Schmidt

*For a Silver Jubilee observance in May, 1910, Cincinnati, Ohio celebrated by draping an enormous flag from the front of City Hall.*